LOS ANGELES

LOS ANGELES

PHOTOGRAPHS BY **TIM STREET-PORTER** INTRODUCTION BY **DIANE KEATON**

DESIGNED AND PRODUCED BY WELCOME BOOKS

RIZZOLI INTERNATIONAL PUBLICATIONS, INC.

NEW YORK

4

5

INTRODUCTION

Driving through the sheer size and diversity of Los Angeles with its relentless innovation, reinvention, and groundbreaking architecture is an out-of-body experience. Linked together by the tedious reality of interconnecting freeways, it's almost as if the car has replaced the old "community center". As we pass thousands of other Angelenos, not only are we unaware of each other, we're unaware of everything that surrounds us. Something is missing as we drive past Bullocks Wilshire, the art deco masterpiece down the street from the deserted Ambassador Hotel, playground to the legendary stars of the '30s; one saved, the other teetering on the edge of extinction. Why don't we care for the places that could unite us? Why do we hurry home to our flat screens where the same buildings we just ignored are offered up as curb appeal in the background of the new episode of *The Shield*? Why do we accept the resounding criticisms that have dogged us from the beginning? Los Angeles, the sorry recipient of our forefathers' legendary dream of revitalizing individualism is empty. Los Angeles, endlessly hovering on the edge of significance, is the lowest form of kitsch. Los Angeles, with its seventy-two suburbs in search of a city, has no center. Where is our center?

It's in our imagination. It's the store shaped like a camera on Wilshire. It's Frank Lloyd

Wright's crumbling Ennis Brown House. It's Jane Mansfield's heart-shaped swimming pool. It's Michael Graves' Mickey Mouse holding up the world of Disney. It's Randy's Donuts. It's the Million Dollar Theater. It's standing in line at Tail o' the Pup, where they still sell hot dogs out of a hot dog. It's in the grotesquely overwrought Italianate villa, the ostentatious Swiss chalet, the thatch-roofed English cottage, and the 1-800 tough shed sitting next to the turnkey McMansion near the cantilevered "wanna be" Cliff May ranch house hanging precariously over a hillside in the Valley. It's our next-door neighbor's cactus garden. It's that sushi restaurant in the strip mall off Highland and Santa Monica Boulevard. It's down the street, and around the corner. It's in the distance it takes to drive from Boyle Heights to the edge of the Pacific Rim. Our center, spread within our parameters and perched at the edge of our extremities, is waiting for us hidden in plain sight.

At the center of our center towers the single-family residence. If the rewards of our ambition have been expressed in the acquisition of happiness in a home, then the hedonistic god that homeowners answer to is Real Estate. For all its legendary landmark status, the Hollywood sign built during the prohibition was nothing more than a huge billboard promoting Harry Chandler's real estate development. Whether we like such shameless promotion or not, the truth is real estate gave architects an opportunity to grow into their potential by fulfilling the whimsy of prospective buyers who believed.

What did Schindler and Lautner and Neutra have to lose in a city where impulse ran rampant? Experimenting with new styles and techniques, the constraints of symmetry and form never stopped anyone in Los Angeles. Not only did this atmosphere realize genius and its potential, but the unlikely alliance of architects, contractors, engineers, buyers, and real estate brokers created the most dizzying array of deviant structures that people call "home" on the face of the earth. Beauty spawned from such fraudulence is all too human. Living in a fantasy of a fantasy based on a dream of a past that never was is forgivable. After all, the results are astonishing.

Tim Street-Porter has created a provocative piece of work with *Los Angeles*. His book has taken a giant step toward balancing the playing field between a public and private Los Angeles. Domestic architecture has always taken precedence over its public institutions, but with persistence fueled by passion Tim Street-Porter has single-handedly connected the dots between our intimate needs and our lagging communal responsibilities. In the thirty years he has documented the soul of Los Angeles with his dazzling images, Tim has driven down more streets of our city than anyone. In that way his book is a search and rescue mission;

a beautiful guide through the peaks and valleys of a valiant architectural wonderland. Tim takes us on a journey that invites us to turn off the white noise of our entertainment centers, call to isolation, turn on our ignitions, and feel the wind on our faces as we put the pedal to the metal and drive.

Accepting Tim's invitation, I head up Mullholland toward the Getty where I can see the grand horizontal thrust of the city below. Looking to the east a larger cluster of skyscrapers dominates our downtown skyline. To the west I see Century City with its 176 high-rises. But what kills is all that lies in between; namely, the overwhelming expanse of one- and two-story structures that, like our forefathers, seem to be rushing to the end of world in search of a dream. I think of dreams. If dreams are nothing more than a series of longings and memories on which to hang a life, then surely these structures still hold the pulse of our forefather's lives within their walls. I think of people: all the people I've passed inside places throughout Los Angeles over the course of a lifetime. I think of the peace I felt as we silently shared the experience of our city's accomplishment together. I think of Los Angeles, where the architecture that marked the milestones of what was envisioned as the future now stands as a legacy to the past. I think of Los Angeles, the appropriation capital of the world, the Wild West of the imagination, the dumping ground for every revamped hybrid ever assembled; I think of it in its entirety, all of it, every acre, every square foot, every inch; Los Angeles, America's premiere landmark city of the twentieth century, my home.

It's sad that my generation has become a metaphor for the endangered twentieth-century landmark about to be traded in for a newer model. As we hand off our contributions, before collecting our gold watches, I have to say letting go isn't nearly as hard as bearing the burden of responsibility for our great city. This falls to the next generation who must be made aware that all eyes will be looking to Los Angeles for what the United States of America will be in the twenty-first century. I hope the leveling of neighborhoods that has brought about the destruction of the past in the name of progress will not overshadow our sons' and daughters' need to lovingly protect the common fate of our landscape. I hope they develop a way of seeing beyond the obvious. Like me, I hope they find themselves driving west on Mullholland, with the wind on their faces. And finally, on behalf of the history of our future, I pray their dreams will include a longing to create new ways to come together in the ever-changing City of Angels, our love.

—DIANE KEATON, June 2005

9

PHOTOGRAPHER'S NOTE

My first visit to Los Angeles was to see The Beatles at the Hollywood Bowl. On the same weekend I also managed to visit all the Frank Lloyd Wright houses that were less deafening but just as eye-opening. My exploration of these successfully offset my initial impression of L.A. as a place both vast and enigmatic: once I got off the freeway and into the hills, the magic began. Every bend on those winding roads opened up new vistas of lush landscaping and houses of every description imaginable, it was almost too exotic and tantalizing for a single weekend. Also, it was unexpected. I had not yet seen David Hockney's paintings of Hollywood apartments and swimming pools, nor had I read British historian Reyner Banham's seminal book, *Los Angeles and the Four Ecologies*, not yet published, which was to brilliantly introduce the diverse wonders of the city to the generations of British architectural students who immediately succeeded mine. Los Angeles, beyond the familiar dimensions of its movie industry, was a sleeping giant waiting to be discovered.

My affinity with America had been locked in place since childhood. Subscription copies of *The Saturday Evening Post* were regularly passed on to me by an American aunt. This was heady material for a child like me, growing up in postwar England—a country in a state of depression and still undergoing food rationing. I was brainwashed by glamorous Technicolor ads for trains (the Santa Fe Super Chief gliding through desert landscapes), cars (new futuristic two-tone models every September), and refrigerators (we made do with a larder) so huge you could walk right into them, loaded with gallon drums of multi-flavored ice cream and enormous hams. This was my vicarious childhood, so when I was offered an exchange program to spend the summer in America from my architectural college, these childhood fantasies resurfaced decisively and said, "Go!" And I did. Noting quickly on arrival that the east coast looked too European, I drove across the country to California and San Francisco, which for me was decisively the "real" America.

It was nearly ten years before I was in L.A. again, in 1973. No longer an architectural student, I was now a photographer, visiting again from England—this time for three months. I produced stories on the Baja 500 car race and James Coburn's house, madly

decorated by Tony Duquette, for *British Vogue*. I was hooked. This time I became more aware of the 50s apartments edged with palm trees, the light, and the vast desert spaces that had attracted Hockney. In 1977 I moved here with Australian artist Annie Kelly. We adored the climate (and who could not, coming from London), the landscape, and the brilliant light. We didn't care that L.A. was in some ways still a cowboy town: the theater, for example, was not exactly the West End, and there were few restaurants (Musso and Franks was tolerable, as long as you ordered the sand dabs). But we didn't care; the sophistications of London had become too predictable anyway. By contrast, the deadpan humor of Ed Ruscha's paintings and early signs of dissonance from architect Frank Gehry, both of whom I had gotten to know, were indications of a non-European cultural edge which drew us to Los Angeles.

My first years in L.A. were spent exploring

and documenting outlying neighborhoods with graphic and unintentionally amusing buildings and signage. There was an innocence in those days which evaporated with the economic boom during the 80s. (This was the decade when corner malls appeared everywhere, replacing those wonderful 50s drive-ins). I was also documenting Frank Gehry's early experiments with new vocabularies in architecture. I remember a visit to New York before he had finished his own house, which was to be his breakthrough with the media, trying to sell a studio he did for artist Ron Davies to Mildred Schmertz, a senior editor at *Architectural Record*. "Dear Frank," she said, looking quizzically at the pictures, "I'm sure we'll get around to publishing him one day."

I have watched L.A. grow into a vibrant metropolis, where, as ever, you do not have to make lifestyle sacrifices to take your place at the trough. Yes, we can ski and surf in the same day (although I never have). Yes, we can see Catalina Island on clear days. We can also live in mid city and grow oranges, avocados, figs, bananas, and loquats in our moderate size garden, as we did at our last house. Both the theatre and the opera are now to be taken seriously and we can enjoy the L.A. Philharmonic at the acoustically amazing Disney Concert Hall. In today's L.A. we can eat in hundreds of sophisticated restaurants, although few are as charming as Musso and Franks where sand dabs are still on the menu.

I have been fortunate to live in Los Angeles, and these photos, taken over the years, are an expression of my love for the city and its unique heritage. *Los Angeles* is my answer to all those who have ever said, including city and county officials on occasion, "There is nothing worth saving here."

—TIM STREET-PORTER, June 2005

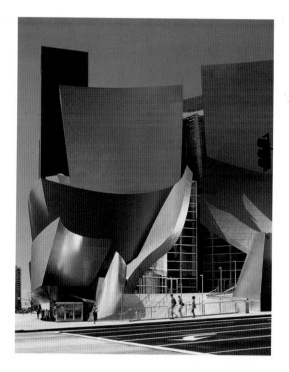

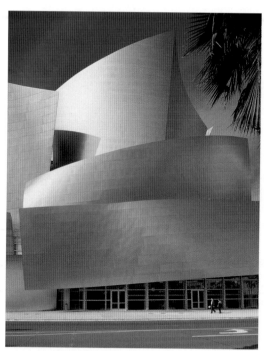

24

36

46

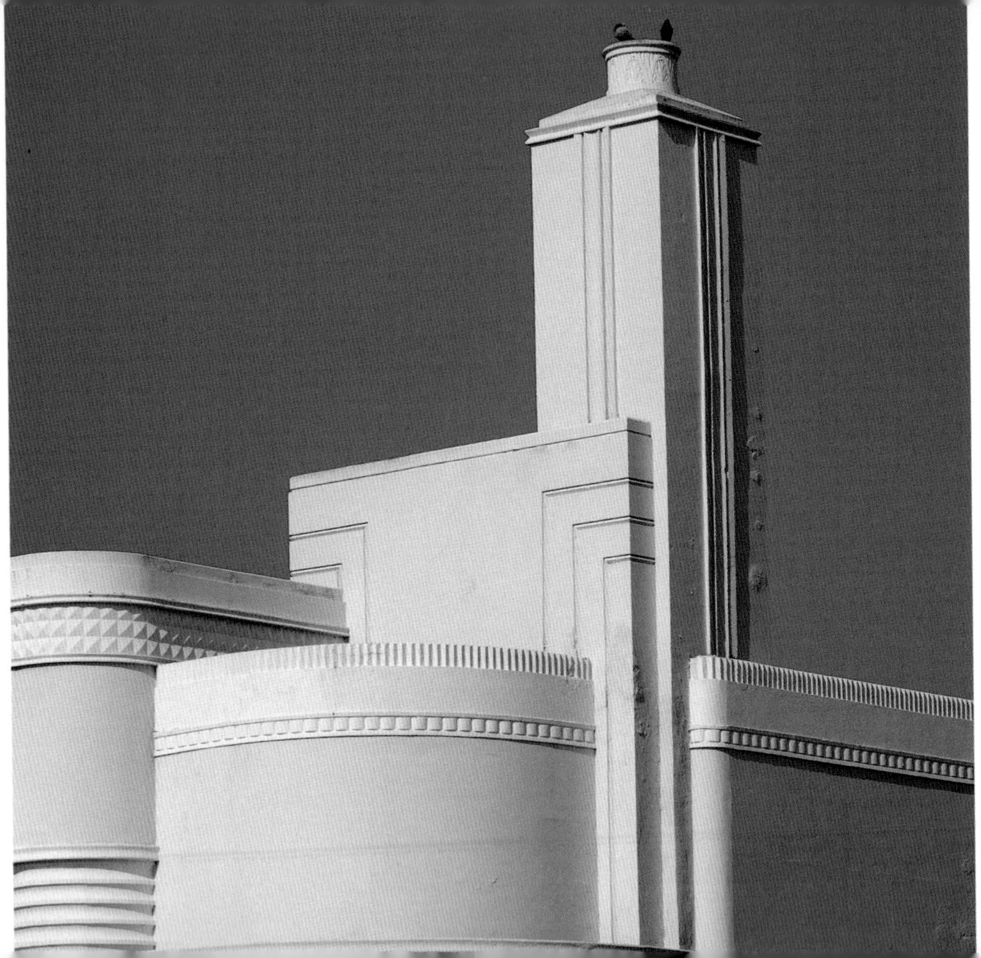

60

61

72

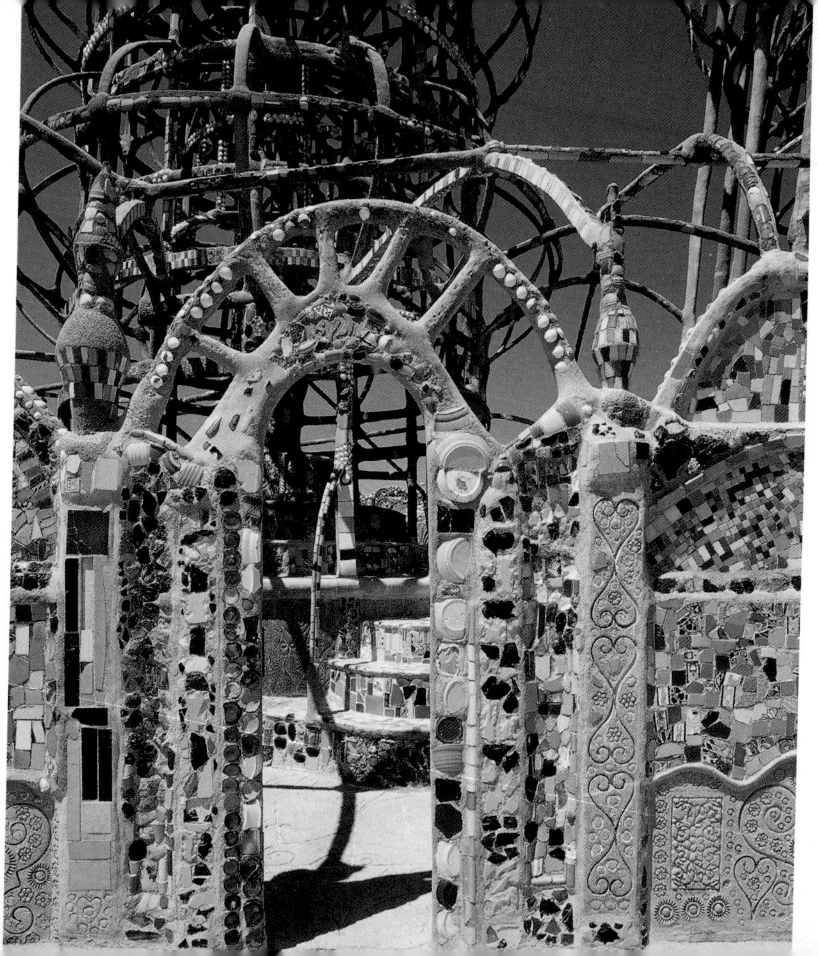

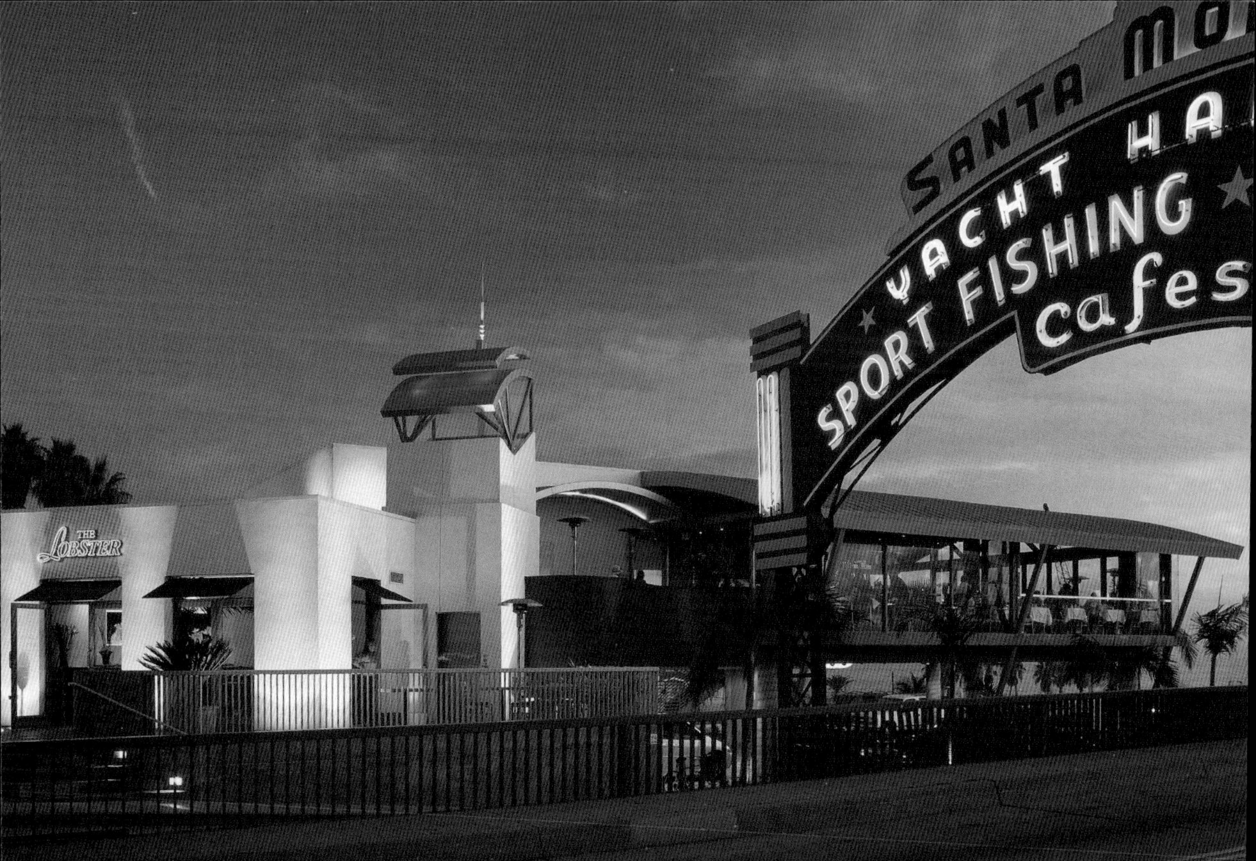
SANTA
YACHT
SPORT FISHING
cafes
THE
LOBSTER

122

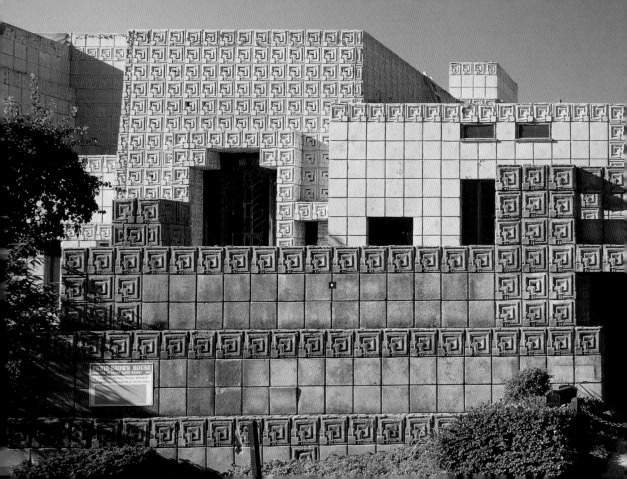

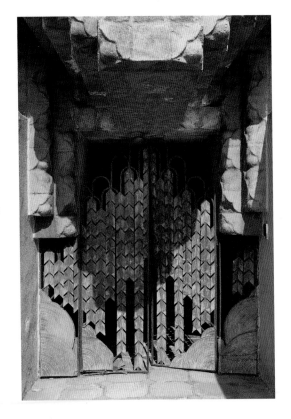

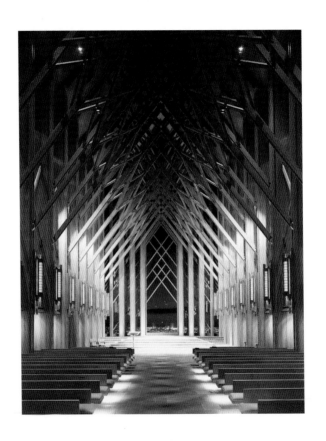

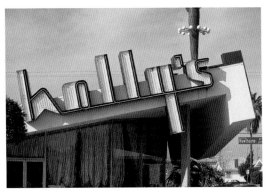

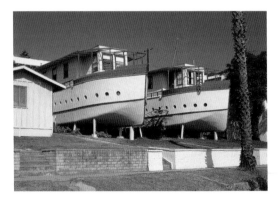

237

INDEX

253

254

255

alterations: Larry Totah; Bel Air Hotel; Levit House (Beverly Hills), Richard Neutra, renovations: Matthew Rolston & Ted Russell; Slatkin residence (Bel Air), Tom Beeton; Gary Cooper residence (Beverly Hills), A. Quincy Jones and Mark Rios; residence (Hollywood), Mark Rios; residence (Altadena), Fung & Blatt.

ACKNOWLEDGMENTS

Special thanks to Charles Miers, publisher at Rizzoli. His enthusiasm for architecture is infectious and was a constant encouragement. It was Charles who gave me this assignment, and it is the most rewarding project I have ever had the opportunity to work on. My editor at Rizzoli, Ilaria Fusina, was always accessible and our collaboration was a pleasure.

Thanks also to Gregory Wakabayashi of Welcome Enterprises, who designed the book so beautifully, and Katrina Fried, his colleague at Welcome, for her organizational skills and hospitality.

I am eternally grateful to all the individuals and institutions who let me photograph their buildings, with no remuneration, recognizing only that it is important to celebrate and support L.A.'s wonderful architectural heritage.

Thanks to my assistant Christin Markmann who helped me with the photography and the production.

With her passion and support for Los Angeles and its treasures, I felt that Diane Keaton was the perfect choice to write the introduction, and I am grateful that she agreed to do so.

I would also like to acknowledge the watchful eyes of the L.A. Conservancy who need our support in their efforts to protect the city's historic buildings.

There are many additional people who helped me with ideas, locations, and contacts, and I am sorry I cannot mention them all individually. Thank you all.

Finally, this book has benefited from the invaluable judgment and support of my wife, Annie Kelly.

First published in the United States of America in 2008 by
Rizzoli International Publications, Inc.
300 Park Avenue South, New York, NY 10010
www.rizzoliusa.com

Rizzoli Editor: Ilaria Fusina

Designed and produced by Welcome Enterprises, Inc.
6 West 18th Street, New York, NY 10011
www.welcomebooks.com

Project Editor: Katrina Fried
Designer: Gregory Wakabayashi

Library of Congress Catalog Control Number: 2007940483

ISBN 978-0-8478-3107-4

2008 2009 2010 / 10 9 8 7 6 5 4 3 2 1

Printed in China